The Ocean of Inspiration

MARYAM YOUSAF

In the name of Allah,
the All-Compassionate and All-Merciful

Muslima Today Publishing

Muslima Today Publishing

www.muslimatoday.com

Dedication

This book is dedicated to every Muslim, to every believer in God who is striving to be better. But most of all, this book is dedicated to my family and to the one who inspires me the most; my Lord, Allah the Almighty.

Table of Contents

Introduction

Life is a journey which returns you to Allah. Sometimes we forget this and become consumed by what life throws at us. If we keep in mind that nothing is coincidental and there is a lesson to be learned in every situation we are placed in; then we are never at a loss.

So no matter where you are in life, or whatever your circumstance, know that you are never alone. Sometimes a simple reminder can give you the inspiration and motivation to carry on and give you the strength to keep striving no matter what. That is why I have written this book, full of inspirational and motivational quotes, so it can remind you and give you the strength and inspiration you need In Sha Allah.

A note to the reader: Although some quotes use she/her/woman pronouns, they are equally applicable to both genders and all people.

Inspirational Quotes

Ocean

Her thoughts were as deep as the
Ocean- full of inspiration, inviting
people to swim in the depths of
her mind.

Bismillah

Every day is a new day, a new chance,
so Bismillah to new beginnings.

Chaos

If you have full faith and tawakkul in Allah,
then even in chaos you will find peace.

Storm

I have the strength to endure every
hardship, I have the power to be
strong during every weak moment
because my Lord assures me that
He does not burden a soul more than
it can bear, and this calms every
storm within me.

Ties

There was a time when I felt I was not good enough, so I held on to those who were not good for me. When people asked me why I held on to people who didn't deserve anything from me, I said it was because I didn't like breaking ties, even though it killed me inside. But today I hold on for a different reason, it makes me feel alive, it's for the Sake of Allah.

Struggles

Despite the struggles, the trials
and disappointments she lives
every day with a beaming smile
because she knows with every
loss there is a gain and with
every hardship there is ease.

Scars

We are haunted by memories,
tainted by scars, yet we are in
charge of what we allow to live
within us. So shut the door to
the ghosts of the past, and seek
protection from the pearls of
prayer.

Run

What you need to realise is,
the people who break you are not
the same people who will mend
your broken heart. What you need
to do is run, run as far away as you
possibly can, because the more further
you are from them, the quicker your
heart will heal.

Allah

If you are hopeless, then find hope in Allah.
If you don't have what it takes, then just put
in what you do have. Work hard, pray hard,
and trust in Allah. Your success doesn't come
from you, it comes from Allah. Believe in
yourself because you have Allah. Success,
happiness, peace, delight is all from Allah.

Free Again

We all make mistakes, we must repent
and ask for forgiveness and just as
importantly forgive ourselves. We need
to do all three to truly be free again.

Reliance

In the end, no matter who you
are and what you have been
through; if you have tried your
best and relied on Allah with
a pure and believing heart then
know that He is the All-Knowing,
and your reward is with Him.

Rose

One day, you will meet a man who will not only buy you flowers but make your life just as fragrant and as beautiful as a rose. And In Sha Allah it won't be long until you have a garden growing of roses, your beautiful little children.

Dreams

Dua – Where dreams come true.

Good Muslim

When someone asked me what
I wanted to be when I grow up,
my reply was always the same
- a good Muslim.

Honour

I love what a Muslim woman
represents, what hijab and
modesty represent, nothing
or no one can compete with
the honour we have been
given.

Fearless

Marry someone who
fears Allah, then you
will having nothing to
fear In Sha Allah.

Happiness

Happiness is knowing
what is to come will
be better than what
has passed.

Ups and Downs

One minute in a warzone,
the next minute in a field
of love, this is the ups
and downs of marriage,
stay strong.

Goodbye

You try and resuscitate the
one that doesn't want to
be saved. You try and bring
back the person that lives
there no more. You have
to say goodbye now, before
you kill yourself trying to save
a lost soul.

Future

It doesn't matter where you've come from,
what matters is where you are going. Look
together to the future, hand in hand, nothing
before it matters.

Love

In Sha Allah one day you will
have the love of a man that
will fall in love with all the
things that you hate about
yourself, and accept you
completely. That man will
be your husband.

Ease

My heart is at ease
knowing Allah is
always with me.

Treasure

Darling, you were made for Jannah
and not for the runways of this
dunya. So guard your modesty, it's
your treasure.

Empty

Maybe we feel so empty inside
because we rely on people instead
of relying on Allah.

Qur'an

Even the ugliest of tongues become
beautiful when the Qur'an is recited.

Survival

I survived because I prayed.

Let Go

There is only one true way
to let go, leave it to Allah
and never look back.

Harm

Haram things will only cause
you harm.

Stop

The moment you stop crying for
the wrong reasons, everything
will be okay.

Justice

I stopped complaining to people
when I realised that it is only Allah
who can give me justice.

Timeless

Timeless beauty is found in the Qur'an.
It has treasures for every situation and
can awaken even the deadest of hearts.

Commitment

What is love without commitment?

Competition

In a marriage, no one should
have to compete with anything
or anyone. A marriage should be
based on acceptance and growth.
You are a team, so don't treat it
like a contest.

Privacy

I have no desire or wish for popularity.
I am what I am, I don't require your
opinion neither do I ask for your
approval. What I do seek is privacy,
my own space, with a selective few.
Popularity is cheap and easy but privacy,
now that is priceless.

Betrayal

Don't ever blame yourself for someone's
betrayal. If a person is going to cheat they
are going to cheat no matter what. So stop
blaming yourself, it wasn't because she was
prettier than you, or more loyal. Don't look
for reasons to justify their behaviour. And
stop asking "Why?" or "What did I do wrong?"
And understand you were good enough, and
you will always be good enough. Do not let
one bad experience destroy you.

Awakening

Have you ever read the Qur'an
or listened to it and just burst
into tears? It's like an awakening
which melts away all the problems
that you thought you had.

Wedding

Don't dream of the perfect wedding
but plan for the perfect marriage.

Battle

The first year will always be the hardest. You will have to fight battle after battle to survive. If you are blessed and especially if you are a good person, then you will definitely be envied. The sad truth is

no one will genuinely be happy for you. You must learn to not let your secrets leave the love nest that you call home. It won't make a difference how long you were together before or how much you think

you understand each other, every person is different after marriage, either better or worse. You will need dua and sabr. Don't plan just your wedding but plan and prepare for your marriage, your future.

Question

You will never need to question the
love of the one that truly loves you.

Unbreakable

Her faith was invincible. As a result of this, she became unbreakable.

Kind

She was the kind of girl that was happy for those who would never be happy for her. She was the kind of girl that would pray for the ones that hurt and forgot her. She was the kind of girl that was concerned about helping others, even when she needed help herself. She was the kind of girl that smiled no matter what. She was the kind of girl who would make dua for anyone that walked by her. She was the kind of girl that lived for the akhirah.

Pressure

I'm not alive to follow every trend
that society puts on me. I am alive
to worship Allah in the best possible
way that I can, and follow the sunnah.
So think whatever you wish, your opinion
doesn't matter.

True Happiness

Think about all the things that if someone
did for you, would make you feel happy.
Now do these things for someone else
to experience true happiness.

The Beginning

You brought me to tears, and these tears
brought me to my knees. The farther away
I got from you, the closer I got into sujood.
So thank you for breaking my heart, it was
just the beginning of a new making. It lead
to a purification of my soul, mind, and heart,
a new beginning. So again, thank you for
breaking my heart.

Hole

Give your whole self to Allah and He will
fix the hole in your heart.

I Am More

I am more than just a number, I am more than just a name, I am more than just a pretty face.

Lost

One day you will realise you were never alone. He was always there with you, even when you were lost. It was Allah who found you when you couldn't even find yourself. He listened to you and guided you every step of the way.

Freedom

Through submission to Allah she found freedom.

Alhamdulillah

Alhamdulillah for what could have been, alhamdulillah for what is. Alhamdulillah for the good and the bad. Alhamdulillah for the prayers that were accepted and for the prayers that went unanswered so that we could be protected. Alhamdulillah for every moment and breath we take and for all the blessings that can never be counted. Alhamdulillah for choosing us to be Muslim. Alhamdulillah for all the favours we cannot deny. Alhamdulillah for the guidance when we were lost, alhamdulillah for Islam.

The Creation

Love is what is between the Creator
and the creation.

The Straight Path

If a person keeps advising, reminding,
and directing you to the straight path;
then my brothers and sisters they are
not on your back, but they are the ones
that have got your back, don't let go
of these people.

Reality

Some people's wish is your reality;
always be grateful.

First Love

One day, Allah is going to send you
so much love. Wherever you will look,
you will see nothing but love. This love
will be in the form of a loving spouse,
the pitter-patter of tiny feet, and good
friends who will be a reminder of Allah's
love and a system of support for you. But
no matter how much love you are sent,
never forget your first love, your parents.
Your world might be filled with love but
never forget to fill their lives with just as
much love, their prayers will always be the
reason behind your success and your path
to Paradise.

Blessing

I had a soft heart, I thought it was a curse
but now I know it's a blessing.

Jealousy

There are some people you will meet that will never be happy for you. Everything you do or achieve will be a source of jealousy for them. They will misinterpret, often intentionally what you say or do. You might do things to please Allah but they may do it for their ego and to compete with you. Don't get angry with these types of people because they are in desperate need of guidance. Make dua for them and leave their fate to Allah, we can remind, but only Allah can guide.

Calamity

Patience is the cure to my pain. This
calamity won't last forever. Faith will
get me through this phase and Allah
will give me better days.

Move On

You've got to move on, you have to believe
what happened, happened for the best. You
have to believe it was Allah's way of protecting
you from harm. So put your trust in Allah and
move on.

Sujood

The harder I fell, the harder I fell into sujood.

Jannah

What if I told you there is a place no
eye has ever seen, no ear has ever
heard nor a human heart can ever
think of? A place Allah has prepared
for His righteous slaves.

Peace

Find peace in repentance.

Recite

You know you have made some progress
when you don't feel right if you haven't
read the Qur'an, when your heart feels
restless to recite and hear the words
of Allah.

Purest Love

There are many reasons which make us
love someone. But the strongest reason
should be to love for the sake of Allah,
and for me that is the truest and purest
love.

Loss

We feel saddened when we lose something
or someone but what we need to remember
is that nothing ever belonged to us, even
we will be returned to Allah.

The All-Seeing

Know that Allah sees it all.

Saved

And sometimes Allah will save you
from your own prayers, from all the
things you thought you wanted,
from all the things you thought you
loved and needed. The things that
were bad for you and would have
destroyed you.

Alive

If you are hurt, in pain but it makes
you turn to Allah, then your heart isn't
dead; it has only just come alive.

Pearls

May your tears become your
pearls in Paradise.

Belief

Do not accept any excuses from yourself; you are far better than you believe. With a bit of patience and effort you can attain anything, just pray and have belief.

Test

Every day is a test and the
world is our exam.

Empire

Be a Muslim, behave like a Muslim
and build your empire in Jannah.

Good Actions

Knowledge without action is a waste.
Increase your knowledge and increase
in good actions to taste the true sweetness
of faith.

Cinderella

The world is my Cinderella
and Jannah is my ball.

Queens of Jannah

We weren't made to be queens of beauty pageants or Miss World. We were made to be the Queens of Jannah, so keep on striving my sisters. Our reward is with Allah.

Beauty

Beauty is in the actions, words and
thoughts of a person whose sole aim
is to please Allah.

Deprived

Sometimes we are deprived in order
to be raised.

Success

If you want success you will have
to make effort *and* pray for it,
you will need to do both.

Mention

Every time you mention Him,
He mentions you.

Escape

Allah is my only escape.

Never Again

When I lost you, I found myself,
I found Allah and never was I lost
again.

Sin

Sometimes you have to look past the sin,
to see the person.

Miracles

I don't believe in magic,
I believe in miracles.

Trials

There is no escape from the
trials of the dunya, so wrap
yourself in patience and prayer.
And hold on to these words:
"Verily with every hardship
comes ease".

Drowning

Sometimes I find myself holding on
to people that are troubled and are
the monsters in their own nightmare.
I find myself reaching out to them, in
the hope that they will change. Slowly
these people start to haunt me with their
devilish ways, it is only then I feel I
have no choice but to let go. If they are
drowning, I can't drown with them. But
I still think of these people, and keep them
in my prayers. May Allah save them from
themselves and give them hidayah and
never let their wicked ways damage us
in any way, shape or form.

Author

The Qur'an is a place in which your
heart will find rest since the author is
its Creator.

Purpose

When I found Allah, I found my purpose.
A beautiful beginning that will never end.

If Only

You silly little girl, you sit here wondering 'if only' or 'what if'. Don't you realise you are opening up the doors to Shaytaan with these thoughts? Don't believe the things you tell yourself at night. What happened, happened for the best. He wasn't for you, you weren't for him, no 'ifs' or 'if only' about it. You feel the pain as if it was as fresh as yesterday and that's okay. You have survived, but you cannot replay the same moment forever. You have the courage to move on, you just need to let go of the past and let Allah do the rest.

Helpers

There are some people that will find
one hundred excuses not to help.
And there are others who will find just
one excuse to help out of one hundred
reasons not to. Which one are you?
Let's change our mentality and be
helpers of one another and when we
call each other 'brothers and sisters'
let's mean it.

Sabr

The key to getting through life is
sabr, sabr, sabr.

Pain

Let your pain help people
not break them.

Wednesday 2018, May,
Day before Ruza.

Sometimes I get angry
and I wanted to take
this out on anyone that
pissed me off slightly.

Popularity

It's not always easy to do the right thing,
it can make you unpopular, so let it be. We
do not seek popularity, but we seek to
encourage good and forbid evil and
ultimately, to please our Creator.

Always

Happiness is knowing no matter
what happens Allah will always
be there.

Fight

If you want a happy and successful marriage, then

you will need to overlook faults and forgive your spouse often. You will have to fight for your marriage to survive. When all you want to do is scream and shout you will need to turn these feelings of rage into tears of release and humble yourself; communicating calmly what it is your heart is aching to say. When things seem impossible, you will need that moment of patience the most. If you want your marriage to survive then you will need to start praying for it now, before there is any difficulty; while you are happy, because one day it's these prayers that will save you.

Mirror

Mirror, Mirror on the wall
who is the most modest of
them all?

Friendship

Friendship and companionship are important in Islam. A good friend is one who accepts your shortcomings, but at the same time guides and supports you. A good friend is one who accommodates your faults and corrects them where possible. A good friend is one who will love and forgive you for the sake of Allah.

Goals

Believers become achievers.
Don't limit yourself by seeking
only the dunya. Real success lies
in aiming for and obtaining Jannah.
Set your goals high.

Healing

My broken pieces have come together, I didn't
think it would happen but I swear, I've healed,
alhamdulillah I've healed.

Strive

It's not a matter of being Muslim,
it's a matter of behaving like one,
and the power you put into
striving to be better.

Girls

Hot girls steal glances,
beautiful girls steal hearts.

Grow

Marry someone that you not only
grow old with but someone you
can grow in faith with.

Comfort

Even in your loneliest moments
you are not alone, Allah is always
with you. You say no one understands.
Tell me, who could understand you
better than the one who created you?
It is Allah that can remove your sorrows
and replace them with happiness.
Allah will be the only one to cure your
pain and give you what you want and
need. Even if you feel weak know
the All Powerful is watching over you,
every time you feel low turn to Him,
only Him. He can provide you with
the comfort the whole world cannot
give you.

Remember

Remember Allah and He will
remember you.

The Words of Allah

I fell in love with the words of Allah
when I understood that it's the only thing
that gives me comfort and ease.

Work

We cannot change the past but we can
do everything to work for a better future.

Gift

If you want to be a better Muslim
then there is no time like the present.
Open this gift and embrace this faith
fully before your time is up.

Instincts

Trust your instincts, do not
blindly follow what your heart
wants you to believe. Listen to
what your head is telling you
to avoid later regrets.

Diamonds

Tears cried in fear of Allah are like
diamonds falling from the eyes.

Heavy Hearts

Heavy hearts like heavy mountains
on your shoulder, are best relieved by
prayer and patience.

Strength

Your strength is your faith in Allah.

True Love

Love is knowing that Allah loves you
and there is no better love than that.

Secret

The secret to healing is in helping others.

River

You were made to cry a river to
wash away the dirt from your
eyes so that you could finally
see clearly.

Lesson

Maybe your situation will change when
your heart learns its lesson and is freed
from the love of the dunya.

God

To be true to yourself is to be
true to God.

Revival

You were alive before you met him.
And you are alive now. Live to worship
Allah, it's the only thing that will revive
your dead soul.

Brave

Brave is the one who in this day and age still forbids evil and enjoins good. Brave is the one, in the age where people are slaves to fashion, strives to obey Allah and to be modest. Brave is the one who doesn't shy away from the commands of Allah but fully submits his or her will to Him. Brave is the one who doesn't care about popularity and will still speak the truth even if their voice shakes. Brave is the person who is often judged as being "judgemental" only because they remind people of their duty to their Creator and convey the message of the last and final Messenger Muhammad (peace be upon him).

Peace

The peace that you are looking
for is in the Qur'an.

The Best

You will try, you will fail.
But the secret to success
is to keep on trying to be a
better person, a better Muslim,
the best possible version of
yourself. You will get there
one day, just start striving now.

First Place

With the dunya you will always
get second place, a new face will
always be ready to replace you.
But with Allah you will always
remain in first place, why
settle for anything less?

Intentions

Big changes come from
small intentions. Make
the niyaah and see your
world change.

Knowledge

Spread a little knowledge
wherever you go.

Modesty

Modesty is a girl's best friend.

Islam

If you were unworthy of Islam
then you would be dead. You
are alive because you have been
given the opportunity to come
back to Allah. Don't let anything
stop you from giving your best.

The only One

The only One that can help you is Allah.
You need to return to Him. No matter
how long it has been since you last prayed,
no matter what sins you are involved in,
take that first step towards Him. The only
One that can take you out of the situation
you are in is Him.

Mistakes

I have learned that my mistakes do not define me. My faith defines me. It doesn't matter how much I have sinned. What matters is that I have repented.

Rumours

Most rumours are started by envious people; or the ones that failed to attain what they wanted. It's best not to react to their callous behaviour. Sooner or later, they will find a new interest.

Qur'an and Sunnah

There are two things that you need in your life the Qur'an and the Sunnah, don't ever be without them.

Reflect

It is strange how advice can be taken negatively, but compliments are taken positively. We choose to listen to what we want to hear, but run away from what needs to be heard. Sometimes, what we love is bad for us and what we hate is good for us. But do we reflect?

Past

You are not your past, maybe you've had some bad experiences and made some bad choices, learn from them and move on.

Never

If only we knew the blessing in helping someone
we would never turn them away.

A Way Out

Once you become conscious of Allah,
He will prepare for you a way out, and
provide for you from sources that you
could never imagine.

Weakest Moments

The truth is, jealous and hateful people
look forward to the moment you slip
up. Once you have repented and sorted
yourself out they cannot bear it. At every
opportunity, they may remind you of your
weakest moments. Do not let them get you
down and never go back to what Allah saved
you from. Leave these people in the pathetic
state that they are in and continue to spread
goodness.

Sacrifices

I thought I was giving things up, but with
all the sacrifices I made, I was only gaining.
When we give something up for the pleasure
of Allah, we never lose.

Fear Allah

If you only fear Allah, then there is
nothing else to fear ever again.

Achieve

Islam brings out the best in me,
it pushes me to achieve things
I never thought I could. Everything
makes sense because of it.

Cracks

It's the cracks that let the light in.

Pray

The beautiful moment when
'I need to pray' becomes
'I want to pray'.

Forgive Yourself

It can be difficult to forgive yourself, but you've got to, you must, it's the only way to move on and become better. So repent, learn, and forgive others and yourself to achieve peace.

Religion

My attitude and actions will never be based
on how you treat me or what you think of
me. My religion taught me better than
that.

Manners

Let your good manners change the world,
but don't let the world change your
manners.

Feel It

The thing about the Qur'an is that you
don't just read it but you feel it. It
touches your soul to the core. I
swear nothing has brought peace to
me like the words of Allah.

Ultimate Strength

I had no one but Allah and this became
my ultimate strength.

Good Things

Good things come to those who pray.

Mother

Her heart is an ocean
full of love; my darling
mother.

Forever

You must be there, when everyone else leaves.

You must believe, when everyone else loses hope.

You must love, when no one else is left to love you.

You've got to have your own back when everyone

turns their back on you. Be there for yourself now,

tomorrow and forever and let God be enough for

you.

Heartache

The dunya will give you nothing but heartache.
People will always try and second guess you.
But if you know in your heart what is true,
you fear Allah and you have good intentions then
as long as it is not harming anybody keep doing
what you are doing, keep going. Don't let
people's praise be your beginning neither
let their criticism be your end.

You and Allah

The beauty of intention is that it
is between you and Allah.

Plans

I plan and Allah plans, but
His plans are always better.

Stones

When the world throws stones
at you; know that if your heart
is pure then Allah's mercy will
lift you up.

Lifestyle

We expect our circumstances to change
while we distance ourselves further away
from the light. We ask when this trial will
end, blinding ourself to the reality that our
lifestyle needs changing.

Duas

Your duas are your diamonds.

Life

A private life is a peaceful life.

Potential

Just because we don't see the potential, it doesn't mean it's not there.

Change

She wished she could change the world
but first she had to change herself.

Allah Alone

The only love that will truly satisfy the heart is from Allah alone.

Relief

There is relief in crying to Allah,
it soothes the soul.

Purpose

Remember your purpose.

Poems

Her Faith

It was her values, her trust, her hope,
her confidence. It was her reason to
love and to never breakdown. It was
the purpose of her life.

In the darkest
of seasons, during the darkest struggles,
it still gave her a million reasons to smile
and be kind.

In it peace she did find.

It was in her speech, her character and
mannerisms. Never did she leave it
behind. Her breath, her strength, her
reason to live.

It was simply her faith
Islam.

Walking Dawah

She was like a walking dawah
she spread the greetings of peace
wherever she went.
Her smile
was the invitation to the truth,
warmth it spread.

Making things
easy, and always helping the needy.

Reminders of Allah and the messages
of the Prophet (salallahu alayhi wa
sallam) is what she sent.

Following
the laws of Allah and the guidance
of her Prophet and helping people
with their shahadah, she was just
like a walking dawah.

The Lord of the Worlds

She didn't need a magic carpet,
she had a Musallah. It took her
to what was better than the whole
world and what was in it. It took her
to where she needed to be.

It took
her to Allah,
the Lord of the Worlds.

That Special Time

It was that special time again.
She was eager and excited to
speak to Him. She wanted to
be at her best so she purified
herself with ablution and put
on her best clothes. She could
feel the love and warmth
surround her. Yes, it was that
special time again. She looked
at the clock and stood in
anticipation until she heard the
call. The call was like sweetness
and honey to her ears. So beautiful
and peaceful, she responded to
His call. She hurried to Him and
prayed. Yes, it was that special
time again, the time for Salah.

Fajr, Zuhr, Asr, Maghrib and Isha.

Princess

He was in search for his perfect
princess. He wasn't just looking
for a wife, but for a mother for his
future children. He understood if
the shoe fits then everything else
would fall into place. After all,
Jannah would lie under her feet.

Heaven on Earth

She woke up and turned towards him.
The door swung open, her children ran
into her arms. It was then she realised
she had found heaven on Earth. She
knew this moment wouldn't last forever
therefore, she made it her prerogative to
ensure that their love for God was greater
than their love for her. She realised one
day she would have to leave. She didn't
feel sad because she understood if they
had Allah that it would be enough for
them, and there was nothing else they
would ever need again.

Safe Haven

She carried him to a place that no one
could reach.

She carried him to a place
that would give him power and protection.

She carried him to a place that would be
his greatest weapon and a safe haven.

She carried him in her dua.

Perfect Prince

The perfect Prince you want to
find. From frog to frog, your heart
will pine. No value for yourself,
your body or your mind. Like a
carcass from place to place you
will find. Meaningless relationships,
your role you can't define. A
girlfriend, a mistress, a pastime.
Friends with benefits, behaving
just like swine. The respect of a
wife you won't find. If you want
happiness, love and be valued in
this lifetime, then expect to change
and live according to the plan of
Allah the Divine. He has raised your
status as a daughter, sister, mother
an equal to mankind. Accept His
will and In Sha Allah bliss you will find.

Eid

The days of Eid, the days the hard hearts soften, the

days foes become friends, the day all is forgotten.

Eid, the days lost relationships are once again bound,

and there are smiles and hugs all around.

The day all

men, children and women are found in Mosque thanking

Allah for all His bounties and keeping them safe and sound.

Eid, the day a miser becomes wiser, even the hardest hearts

are awoken. Gifts, money, eidi, giving in charity and joining

in the celebrations people of all colours and backgrounds.

Never denying the favours of their Lord praising Him with

Takbeer - Allahu Akbar Allahu Akbar Allahu Akbar Wa-lil-Lahil hamd.

Reading Eid Salah, and praising Him night and day.

Alhamdulillah for Eid.

Ramadan

The long nights of Ramadan were like no
other. After breaking their fast they would
sit next to each other holding their hands up
in dua, beseeching their Lord. He would then
pull her up from her Musallah and hand her
the Qur'an. He would recite from hers,
she would recite from his so that they could
increase their ajr. She would cook him iftar
and he would serve her suhoor. And that is
how they would spend their nights together
in worship, they were the most romantic
nights of their life.

Dawah

Dawah to me is like breathing
I can't give up until they start
believing.

Never any force
only tender words to reinforce
the truth, the only truth.

God
is one, come to Him.
Honestly
it's the only healing for your
human bleeding.

Save Me

"O Allah save me, save me,
save me!" she cried, little
did she know that this was
her secret to being saved.

Pure Love

She met him when she was at
her lowest. When she thought
no one would want her, when
she thought she was unlovable.
He gave her hope when she was
hopeless. She knew he was the
one and he was different when
he sent his parents for her hand
and to express his love. Since
that day, her life was never the
same again. She learned a very
important lesson, that Allah will
sometimes send you pure love
when you aren't looking for it
but are in most need of it.

Most Beautiful

He found her most beautiful
not when she was all dolled
up, with her hair perfectly
straight, but when she wore
her hijab. He found her most
beautiful not when she wore
the little black dress but when
she wore her long black abaya.
He was proud of her, not when
all eyes were on her, but when
she only allowed his eyes to be
on her. He found her most
beautiful when she was simple,
when she stood on her prayer
mat and answered the call to
Allah. She was extremely
beautiful, but he didn't find her
most beautiful because of her
looks, but for her commitment
to Allah and for her one-of-a-kind
character.

She Wasn't Perfect

She wasn't perfect, she never claimed
to be. But she was honest and truthful
just the way her Prophet (peace be
upon him) told her to be. Her thoughts
were on her tongue, grudges she refused
to keep. Always trying to see the best in
people so that maybe Allah would only see
the best in her.

Spotlight

They asked "Why do you cover?"
She replied "Because I don't need
that kind of attention. People that
shine don't need the spotlight".

The Beauty of her Faith

She was always told that there was
something about her, they could
never put their finger on it. But
she knew what it was, it was Allah's
infinite mercy on her and the beauty
of her faith.

All My Life

"Where have you been all my life?" she asked.
He smiled and replied "In your duas".

Secret Whispers

Her duas were the secret whispers
of her heart being translated into
prayers.

Thank You

As she finished off her prayer
she cried "O Allah thank you
for always listening to me,
even though I don't always
listen to you".

Broken Pieces

She placed her trust in Allah and moved
on with her life. She gathered all of her
broken pieces; the tears, and all of her
fears and left them in sujood. She knew
only Allah could put them back together
again and fix what was left broken in her.
Despite of all her sorrow she would remind
herself that it wasn't good to dwell on the
past. It was difficult at first but slowly it
became easier.

Priority

She made Allah her priority and occupied
her time in doing good deeds. She made
dua as she knew this was her weapon against
negative feelings and thoughts. It wasn't
long until she healed beautifully.

Allah's Plan

Everything that she had known
she had left behind. The new
environment around her was
hostile. She felt isolated and
all alone. She spent a couple
of years in despair but if you
ask her now she would look
back and smile with utter joy
because she saw the beauty
of Allah's plan unfold.

Broken

He broke her. He broke her trust,
he broke her dreams, he broke his
promises. He broke her confidence,
he broke her self-esteem. He nearly
broke her heart. Her heart was safe
you see, it wasn't completely his to
break. It belonged to Allah alone and
her love for Him was greater than any
created being. So, she rebuilt her
dreams, confidence and self-esteem.
She rebuilt her trust, relationships and
everything. Broken again she would
never be. She now depended on
something unbreakable, her faith
in Allah, the Supreme.

Tears

Finally, the tears that hit her face
like huge waves had washed away
her sorrow. It took years of pain
but she was ready to live her life
again like there was no tomorrow.
That's what happens when you
have patience, faith and live your
life with grace.

Forever in Jannah

His heart and her heart were never to part,
today in dunya and forever in Jannah.

Afterword

Whoever has not thanked people, has not thanked Allah. So, thank you to everyone who has inspired me, supported me and prayed for me, I truly am grateful. JazakAllahu Khayran.

A Brief Glossary of Islamic Terms

Abaya – A full-length, outer garment

Ajr - Reward

Akhirah – Afterlife

Alhamdulillah – All the praises and thanks be to God

Allah - God

Bismillah – In the name of God

Dawah – Call/Invitation

Dua – Supplication

Dunya - World

Eid - A Muslim festival

Eidi – A gift given on Eid

Haram – Forbidden or proscribed by Islamic law

Hidayah – Guidance

Hijab - Veil, Curtain, Partition, Separation. Commonly referred to as a head covering

In Sha Allah - God willing /If Allah wills

Iftar – Meal to break the fast

Jannah – Paradise

JazakAllahu Khayran – May Allah reward you with goodness

Madrassa – A Muslim School

Musallah - Prayer Mat

Muslim – One who submits to God alone

Niyaah - Intention

Qur'an – The Islamic sacred book, the word of God

Ramadan - The annual period of fasting

Sabr – Patience / Endurance

Salah – Prayer performed five times a day (Fajr, Zuhr, Asr, Maghrib, Isha)

Salallahu alayhi wa sallam – May Allah send blessings and peace be upon him.

Shahadah – The Muslim testimony of faith

Shaytaan - Satan

Suhoor – Pre-dawn meal consumed in Ramadan

Sujood - Prostration

Sunnah – The Prophet's (peace and blessings be on him) sayings, actions or tacit approvals

Takbeer – Words used to praise God

Tawakkul –The Islamic concept of reliance on God or "trusting in God's plan", God-consciousness

29661141R00107

Printed in Great Britain
by Amazon